POOCH CAFÉ

POOCH CAFÉ

ALL DOGS NATURALLY KNOW HOW TO SWIM

by Paul Gilligan

**Andrews McMeel
Publishing**

Kansas City

03 04 05 06 07 BBG 10 9 8 7 6 5 4 3 2

ISBN: 0-7407-3302-8

Library of Congress Control Number: 2002111033

───── **ATTENTION: SCHOOLS AND BUSINESSES** ─────

Andrews McMeel books are available at quantity discounts with bulk purchase for educational, business, or sales promotional use. For information, please write to: Special Sales Department, Andrews McMeel Publishing, 4520 Main Street, Kansas City, Missouri 64111.

To Mom and Dad, for always straining the mushroom soup.

DUE TO THEIR RELATIVELY INEXPRESSIVE FACES, JUDGING A DOG'S MOOD CAN OFTEN BE DIFFICULT. THEREFORE, FOR YOUR CONVENIENCE, WE HAVE INCLUDED IN THE FOLLOWING SCENE *WEATHER SYMBOLS* THAT APPROPRIATELY REFLECT THE DOG'S MOOD AT THAT MOMENT.

13

"BEWARE OF DOG"? BUT THAT WOULD IMPLY TO THE BURGLARS THAT I'M SOME SORT OF THREAT. I COULDN'T HURT A FLY.

I SUPPOSE I COULD TALK DOWN TO THEM. HURT THEIR SELF-ESTEEM.

PUT "BEWARE OF CONDESCENDING DOG."

DO YOU NEED HELP SPELLING THAT WORD?

SEE? I'M GOOD AT THAT.

JUST PRACTICE BARKING AND GROWLING, OKAY?!

THAT SIGN HAS GOT "THERAPY" WRITTEN ALL OVER IT.

BEWARE OF DOG

IT SEEMS TO ME YOU'RE LACKING IN SELF-CONFIDENCE. I THINK IT'S TIME WE GOT YOU SOME EMPOWERMENT.

REALLY?

GUARD DOG TRAINING

CHARGE PONCHO

WITH INCISORS LIKE MINE I'M PRETTY SURE I SHOULD BE EATING MORE MEAT.

BULK KIBBLE

PONCHO

I SHOULD BE STALKING GAZELLE OR ZEBRA ACROSS THE SERENGETI, CHASING THEM DOWN IN A FEROCIOUS, PACK-DRIVEN FEEDING-FRENZY.

AND THOSE SQUIRRELS WHO MANHANDLED YOU IN THE BACKYARD?

THAT WAS NO FAIR, THEY WERE TICKLING!

BULK KIBBLE

24

26

28

IT'S STRANGE. THE CATS AND I CAN'T UNDERSTAND EACH OTHER, BUT YOU AND I CAN.

I'M SPEAKING "DOG."

REALLY? CAN YOU SPEAK "CAT," TOO?

FLUENTLY.

GREAT! THEN YOU CAN TRANSLATE THIS CAT CONVERSATION I TOOK DOWN.

WHAT DOES "MEOW" MEAN?

"BITE ME."

GARBAGE DAY TOMORROW, PONCHO. WOULD YOU PLEASE TAKE OUT THE TRASH?

I DON'T THINK IT SHOULD BE PUT OUT THE NIGHT BEFORE. A DOG MIGHT GET INTO IT.

I DON'T ASK YOU TO DO MUCH AROUND HERE, DO I?

ALL RIGHT, I'LL DO IT NOW!

PONCHO!

WELL, I WARNED YOU!!

WE CAN'T GET INTO MOVIE THEATERS OR CONCERT HALLS! WE CAN'T VOTE OR DRIVE CARS!

WE CAN'T GET PASSPORTS OR LIBRARY CARDS! WE CAN'T HOLD DOWN JOBS OR GET AN EDUCATION!

WELL, WE'RE NOT GOING TO TAKE IT ANYMORE! TODAY BEGINS THE REVOLUTION! SOON WE MARCH ON PARLIAMENT WITH OUR DEMANDS ECHOING THROUGH THE LAND!!

BOY, HE REALLY WANTS TO SEE THAT NEW JACKIE CHAN MOVIE.

BIG TIME.

GRRR!!

HEE HEE HA HA HOO!
HEE HA HA HAW HOHA! HA!

OF COURSE YOU'RE NOT SCARY, THE WAY YOU LOOK. YOUR POSTURE IS MEEK AND UNASSUMING WITHOUT A TRACE OF MENACE.

YOU'VE GOT TO CONVEY A MORE INTIMIDATING PRESENCE, PONCHO. IT'S ALL IN THE ATTITUDE.

BEWARE OF DOG

36

TO BE HONEST, I DON'T SEE WHAT THE POINT OF BURYING BONES IS, BUT I HAD TO TRY IT.

WHACK WHACK WHACK WHACK

PONCHO, WHY DON'T YOU JUST CLEAN UP THE WATER?!

ARE YOU SURE IT'S SAFE FOR PONCHO TO ROAM FREE ON THE STREETS?

DON'T WORRY, I WENT OVER THINGS WITH HIM. PONCHO IS CAR SMART.

...AND THE LX MODEL IS KNOWN FOR ITS FAULTY PISTON RINGS, SO CHECK THE OIL FREQUENTLY...

39

ALL-NIGHT FAST FOOD.

SO SINCE CARMEN'S LAME NOW, WILL YOU BE GETTING A NEW MATE?

WHAT? NO, OF COURSE NOT!

BUT IT'S SURVIVAL OF THE FITTEST! SHE'S MAIMED!

IT'S JUST A SPRAINED ANKLE!

THAT'S DEATH IN THE WILD! NATURE MUST CULL THE GENE POOL!

IF SOMEONE GETS LAID UP WITH AN INJURY, WE DON'T JUST CAST THEM TO THE WOLVES! WE'RE CIVILIZED BEINGS!

WELL, SHE SHOULD AT LEAST FORFEIT HER RETIREMENT SAVINGS!

NO, PONCHO, WE'RE NOT LEAVING CARMEN OUT FOR THE WOLVES JUST BECAUSE SHE HURT HER ANKLE.

IT'S NOT WISE TO DEFY THE EVOLUTIONARY PROCESS.

HUMANS STICK BY EACH OTHER. I ALREADY HELPED HER THROUGH HER BOUTS WITH PNEUMONIA, BOTULISM, JAUNDICE AND A SLIPPED DISK.

GEEZ, THIS CHICK'S A LEMON.

ALL RIGHT, OUTSIDE!

SO YOU'RE SAYING THAT HUMANS NEVER REMOVE AILING MEMBERS FROM THE GENE POOL. IN ESSENCE, THEN, EVOLUTION IS DEAD.

OH, WHAT ABOUT YOU, MR. DISCOVERY CHANNEL? DO YOU THINK YOU'D LAST ONE DAY OUT IN THE WILD? WHAT SPECIAL SKILLS HAS EVOLUTION GIVEN YOU?

BALANCING A SPOON ON YOUR NOSE WON'T PLAY ON THE SERENGETI, PAL!

43

45

WHOOPS, SORRY, MIND THE LEASH THERE...

PONCHO, QUIT WRAPPING AROUND... PARDON US... PONCH...

OH, GEEZ... PONCHO, STOP... I'M REALLY SORRY ABOUT THIS...

PONCHO, DON'T DO THAT ANYMORE! I'M MARRIED NOW!

SORRY. OLD TRAINING.

THESE CONTAINERS ARE FOR STORING LEFTOVERS.

"LEFTOVERS"?

YOU KNOW, WHEN YOU HAVE LEFT-OVER FOOD.

HUH?

WHEN YOU HAVE SOME FOOD AND YOU CAN'T FINISH ALL OF IT, AND YOU WANT TO KEEP THE REST FOR LATER!

YOUR MOUTH IS FORMING WORDS THAT I KNOW, BUT PUT TOGETHER IN THAT ORDER THEY HAVE NO MEANING.

JUST FORGET IT.

PONCHO! DO YOU HAVE TO EAT SO FAST? IT'S DISGUSTING!

GOBBLE CHOKE GHAM GLOB

PONCHO

DOGS HAVE TO GORGE THEMSELVES BECAUSE THEY'RE NEVER SURE WHEN THEY'LL EAT AGAIN.

WHAT ARE YOU TALKING ABOUT? YOU EAT AT 7:30 A.M. AND 6 P.M. SHARP EVERY DAY!

MAY 17, 1998. FIFTY-FIVE MINUTES LATE.

I WAS IN A MULTICAR PILE UP!!

...THE TABLES HAVE TURNED, NOW PONCHO'S RUNNING *AWAY* FROM THE SQUIRREL.

THE SQUIRREL HAS GOT HIM DOWN. HE'S GOT HIS KNEES ON PONCHO'S BICEPTS, PINNING HIM.

HE'S RIPPING UP GRASS AND DROPPING IT IN PONCHO'S FACE, LAUGHING AND TAUNTING HIM.

I'M GOING TO HAVE TO START WALKING PONCHO WITH A BAG OVER MY HEAD.

NOW HERE COMES THE SQUIRREL'S MOTHER.

CHECK THIS OUT! WHEN I PUSH AGAINST YOU, YOU AUTOMATICALLY PUSH BACK!

HA! HA! YOU'RE RIGHT!

YOU DO IT, TOO!

WE CAN'T HELP IT! IT'S SOME SORT OF DOG INSTINCT!

WHAT HAPPENS WHEN YOU PUSH AGAINST CATS?

SHOVE

PLOP!

ZIP-A-DEE DO-DAH

WHAT ARE YOU SO HAPPY ABOUT?

GREAT NEWS, OL' BUDDY! I JUST CONFIRMED OUR CAMPING EXCURSION UP THE SIDE OF MOUNT FURIOUS! A FULL WEEK OF JUST YOU AND ME AGAINST THE ELEMENTS! PACK YER BAGS!

FUNERAL MARCH

THE MONTHLY CATAPULT MEETING WILL NOW COME TO ORDER.

AS YOU CAN SEE, I'VE BEEN MAKING SOME REFINEMENTS TO THE DRAWING. I'VE PUT SOME SHADING ON THE WHEELS AND ADDED SOME LANDSCAPE.

I HAVE A QUESTION.

YES, HUDSON?

WHAT KIND OF SHRUBS ARE THOSE SUPPOSED TO BE? 'CAUSE IF THEY'RE SUPPOSED TO BE HYDRANGEAS--

IT DOESN'T MATTER!

LOOK, IT'S SUPPOSED TO BE A FORSYTHIA... OR SOMETHING FROM THE JUNIPER FAMILY, BUT WHO CARES?

AS LONG AS WE'RE PREOCCUPIED WITH SUCH TRIVIALITIES, WE'RE NEVER GOING TO RID THE EARTH OF SMELLY CATS! AM I RIGHT OR AM I RIGHT? WELL?

I TAKE IT FROM YOUR SILENCE YOU ALL CONCUR. SO LET'S PROCEED.

THOSE BIRDS ARE LAUGHABLE.

60

SURE, YOU CAN BED DOWN IN MY FIELD IF YA LIKE.

BUT I RECKON YOU'D BE MORE COMFORTABLE SPENDIN' THE NIGHT IN OUR SPARE ROOM.

MY ONLY RULE IS YA GOTTA KEEP YER HANDS OFF MY DAUGHTER.

I DIDN'T WANT TO BECOME A CHEAP PUNCHLINE.

YOU JUST SAT IN A COW PIE.

GASP... CAN'T WE... TAKE A BREAK? I'M... DYIN'...

OK, MR. COMPLAINER.

GOOD. NOW I CAN CATCH MY BREATH AND READ MY BOOK A BIT.

YOU BROUGHT "WAR AND PEACE" BACKPACKING?!!

I'M REALLY ENGROSSED IN IT RIGHT NOW. I COULDN'T LEAVE IT BEHIND!

BUT WE'LL BE HIKING FOR A WEEK!

HHN... PONCHO... SLAP

"AND TO RECOGNIZE A DEPENDENCE OF WHICH WE ARE NOT CONSCIOUS."

THE END.

BOY, THAT WIND IS REALLY PICKING UP!

YOU HAMMERED IN ALL THOSE TENT PEGS LIKE I ASKED YOU, RIGHT, PONCHO?

PONCHO?

HANG ON, I'M FORMULATING MY ANSWER.

63

73

BOY, THEY'RE REALLY NARROWING THE MARKET WITH THOSE THINGS.

CHICKEN SOUP FOR PONCHO'S SOUL

DID YOU HAVE ANY OTHER SERIOUS RELATIONSHIPS BEFORE ME?

UH OH...

WELL, COME ON, CARMEN! I DIDN'T JUST APPEAR ON THIS EARTH THE DAY I MET YOU. I HAVE A PAST!

YOU UNDERSTAND, DON'T YOU?

YEAH, I DO. SORRY ABOUT THAT.

WHEW! I THOUGHT I WAS IN TROUBLE THERE FOR A--

DID YOU HAVE ANY OTHER DOGS BEFORE ME?

HONEY, CAN YOU TAKE THIS BAG OF SCRAPS OUT TO THE MULCH PILE, PLEASE?

SURE, CARMEN.

CHOMP CHOMP

"MULCH" PILE... I THOUGH IT WAS CALLED THE "MUNCH" PILE.

PONCHO, GET OUT OF THERE!

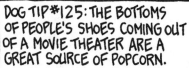

77

79

WELL, I'M VERY DISAPPOINTED IN YOUR LACK OF RESPONSE DURING THE ROBBERY, PONCHO!

HOW COULD YOU BE DISAPPOINTED? WHAT POSSIBLE INDICATION HAVE I EVER GIVEN YOU THAT I WOULD ACT ANYTHING LESS THAN MEEK AND COWARDLY IN A CRISIS SITUATION? DO YOU *KNOW* ME AT *ALL*??

AND ANOTHER THING, YOU KNOW I PREFER LIVER-FLAVORED DOG FOOD, YET STILL YOU BUY--

HEY, *I'M* SUPPOSED TO BE LECTURING *YOU*!!

GUARD-DOG TRAINING?! *ME*?!

THAT'S RIGHT, PONCHO. WE NEED TO PROTECT THE HOUSE FROM BURGLARS.

HOW COME *I* HAVE TO GET GUARD TRAINING BUT NOT THE *CATS*?!

BECAUSE THEY'RE TOO STUPID FOR THE TRAINING.

HAH. I *KNEW* IT!

HOW LONG WILL THAT HOLD HIM?

TIL HE FINDS OUT WE HAVE TO GET UP AT 7:30 A.M.

GREAT

NOW MY MASTER HAS SIGNED ME UP FOR *TRAINING*.

YOU SHOULD COUNT YOURSELF LUCKY. EDUCATION IS A VERY IMPORTANT THING. TAKE ME, FOR EXAMPLE. I--

IF THIS IS LEADING UP TO SOME CRACK ABOUT SPENDING YOUR LIFE IN A *SCHOOL*, I'LL FLUSH YOU DOWN THE TOILET.

I'LL BE GOOD.

84

You see, Poncho, your guard dog training is to stop *HOME INTRUDERS*, not people you consider intrusive in your life...

So, Poncho, you completed guard dog school?

YUP.

Okay, well I'll be back in a sec. Guard my donut for me, will you?

YOU HAVE MY OATH.

GULP

IS HE ON MEDICATION OR WHAT?

THIS PREMISES GUARDED BY CERTIFIED WATCH DOG

?

WHO-- YOU!

OH, YEAH.

THE DAY PONCHO FOUND OUT THAT CATS HAVE NINE LIVES

THIS IS THE MOST TERRIBLE MOMENT OF MY LIFE! I'M SCREAMING ALONG ON A BIKE, TOTALLY OUT OF CONTROL! I'M ABSOLUTELY TERRIFIED!!

AND I'M HUNGRY.

I'M CAREENING DOWN A STEEP HILL ON A BIKE TOTALLY OUT OF CONTROL. I WONDER HOW THIS WILL END UP?

CRASH!

CRASH!

WOW, JUST LIKE I PREDICTED! I'M PSYCHIC!

LOOK AT THE MESS A COUPLE OF RACCOONS MADE WHILE I WAS OUT LAST NIGHT!

MRS. POTTER FROM NEXT DOOR SAW THEM. SHE SAID THEY SEEMED TO BE DELIBERATELY TRYING TO MAKE AS MUCH MESS AS POSSIBLE!

IF I EVER GET MY HANDS ON THOSE RACCOONS THEY'LL BE SORRY THEY WERE EVER BORN!

WE GOTTA BURN THESE COSTUMES.

98

DID YOU KNOW THAT ON HALLOWEEN EVERYONE GETS DRESSED UP AND THEY GIVE OUT FREE CANDY?

YEAH, BUT APPARENTLY THEY DON'T LET DOGS IN ON IT!

WHAT A GREAT DINNER!

SURE WAS! BUT IT'S REALLY LATE NOW, SO LET'S BE REALLY QUIET.

I'LL STICK THE LEFTOVERS IN THE FRIDGE AND SEE YOU UPSTAIRS.

OKAY.

THAT ONE OF THEM SO-CALLED "DOGGY BAGS" YOU GOT THERE?

CLICK

PONCHO, CAN YOU PUSH ME OVER IN FRONT OF THE TV AGAIN?

OKAY, BUT I'M TELLING YOU, BOOKS ARE FAR MORE ENLIGHTENING. TELEVISION ROTS YOUR BRAIN. IT'S TOTALLY MIND-NUMBING AND DANGEROUS AND--

-KRASH!

SEE, NOW LOOK WHAT TV DID!

OH NO! I ACCIDENTALLY PUSHED FISH AND HIS FISHBOWL DOWN THE BASEMENT STAIRS!

BUT I'M TERRIFIED TO GO DOWN AND HELP HIM! IT'S TOTALLY DARK DOWN THERE AND, OF COURSE, THERE'S THE BOOGIE MAN POTENTIAL.

FISH?

CAN YOU GET THE LIGHT SWITCH?

THE DEXTERITY OF A DOG'S TONGUE IS AN AMAZING THING, CAPABLE OF SUCH PRECISION ACTS AS DETECTING A PILL THE MASTER HAS HIDDEN IN A COCKTAIL WEINER AND REJECTING IT WHILE RETAINING THE MEAT. LET'S WATCH IT IN ACTION.

HERE YA GO, BUDDY!

FOREIGN ELEMENT DETECTED!

ALL RIGHT, TEAM! LET'S GO!

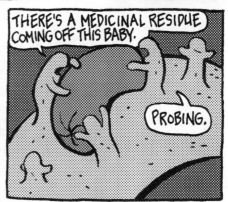

THERE'S A MEDICINAL RESIDUE COMING OFF THIS BABY.

PROBING.

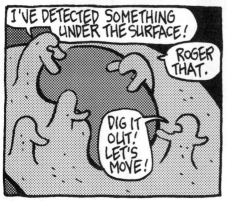

I'VE DETECTED SOMETHING UNDER THE SURFACE!

ROGER THAT.

DIG IT OUT! LET'S MOVE!

GOT IT! IT'S A PILL OF SOME SORT!

REMAINDER OF FOOD CLEAR!

SEND IT DOWN! EJECT THE PILL!

P-TUI

HOW THE HECK DO YOU *DO* THAT?

BY THE AGE OF 30 THE AVERAGE NORTH AMERICAN MALE HAS TWO POUNDS OF UNDIGESTED RED MEAT IN HIS STOMACH.

THE NEIGHBOR'S CAT IS OUT THERE DIGGING IN THE FLOWER BED AGAIN! WELL, I'VE HAD IT!

RELEASE THE HOUNDS!

THAT'S YOUR CUE.

OH YEAH, RIGHT.

YOU RAPSCALLIONS! GET OUT OF MY MASTER'S TRASH BEFORE I SUMMON A CONSTABLE!

CHILL OUT, BUB. WHAT'S THE HARM IN US DOING A LITTLE GARBAGE PICKING?

YOU NOXIOUS, VILE CRETINOUS VERMIN! YOU DON'T EVEN HAVE ENOUGH COUTH TO BE ASHAMED OF ROUTING THROUGH ANOTHER'S REFUSE!

OH-HO! WHAT HAVE WE HERE? "WORM MEDICATION."

THAT DOES IT! I'M ALERTING THE AUTHORITIES!

IT WOULD BE SO GREAT TO HAVE THIS EASY CHAIR AT THE POOCH CAFÉ.

YOU SAID IT.

ALL WE'D HAVE TO DO IS DRAG IT ACROSS THE TOWN SOMEHOW.

YEAH.

IF ONLY WE HAD SOME CREATURES WE COULD HARNESS TO IT AND HAVE THEM PULL IT, LIKE A... LIKE A...

LIKE A SLED?

EXACTLY!

IT'S A NEW GAME PONCHO AND I MADE UP CALLED "DOG SLED."

WE'LL DO ODDS 'N' EVENS TO SEE WHO GETS TO PULL THE "SLED" FIRST. READY?

ODD.

ODD.

EVEN!

HA HA! HA! HEH.

WAIT A MINUTE...

IF WE WANT TO HAUL THIS OLD CHAIR ACROSS TOWN WE SHOULD PUT SOME WHEELS UNDER IT.

LIKE THIS?

THAT'S PERFECT! LET'S GET THE CHAIR ON TOP OF IT!

OKAY, START PUSHING IT... NICE AND EASY... NICE AND EASY...

HOW LONG DO YOU THINK BEFORE WE'RE CHASING THIS THING DOWN A STEEP HILL?

119